MUHAMMAD ALI

MATT CHRISTOPHER®

The #1 sports series for kids

★ LEGENDS IN SPORTS ★

MUHAMMAD ALI

Text by Glenn Stout

LITTLE, BROWN AND COMPANY

New York ᴗ Boston

Little, Brown and Company

Time Warner Book Group
1271 Avenue of the Americas, New York, NY 10020
Visit our Web site at www.lb-kids.com

www.mattchristopher.com

First Edition

Matt Christopher® is a registered trademark of
Matt Christopher Royalties, Inc.

Text by Glenn Stout

Library of Congress Cataloging-in-Publication Data

Stout, Glenn.
    Muhammad Ali / text written by Glenn Stout. — 1st ed.
      p.   cm. — (Matt Christopher legends in sports)
    ISBN 0-316-10843-X
    1. Ali, Muhammad, 1942– — Juvenile literature.   2. Boxers (Sports) —
United States — Biography — Juvenile literature.   I. Christopher, Matt.
II. Title.   III. Series.

GV1132.A4S86   2005
796.83'092 — dc22   2004007568

10 9 8 7 6 5 4 3 2 1

COM-MO

Printed in the United States of America

Contents

★ CHAPTER ONE ★

1942–1954

Birth of the Greatest

Muhammad Ali may be the most recognized man in the entire world.

From the United States to Africa, Asia, and Europe, boxing champion Muhammad Ali remains the most popular and best-known athlete of the last fifty years. More than twenty years after his last bout, wherever Ali goes fans of all colors, religions, and nationalities mob him. They recognize him simply as the Greatest.

But over the course of his remarkable life, Muhammad Ali has become known for far more than his athletic accomplishments. He is a symbol of personal courage and conviction. Since retiring from boxing, and despite serious illness, the former world champion has preached peace, tolerance, and understanding among the many peoples of the world. "All great men are tested by God," he has said. If that is true, then the life of Muhammad Ali contains lessons for all.

No one could have possibly foreseen that the young Muhammad Ali would become such an important athlete. There was absolutely nothing about his childhood or upbringing that made him stand out. The name Muhammad Ali did not even exist yet. The man who would eventually be known by that name started out with another.

On January 17, 1942, Odessa Clay gave birth to a boy. His parents named their first son after his father, Cassius Marcellus Clay.

Cassius Clay Sr. was a painter in Louisville, Kentucky, a talented and flamboyant man who liked to work hard and have fun. He was able to support his family by painting signs, billboards, and murals in local churches. As far as it can be determined — for family records are incomplete — Cassius senior's ancestors were what were once known as "free coloreds," people of African descent who were not slaves. But it is likely that at some point in the past his ancestors were slaves in the American South. More than a few plantation owners and slaveholders were named Clay, and slaves often took on the last name of their master.

Ali's father, in fact, was named after a white man. In the middle of the nineteenth century, just before the Civil War, a man named Cassius Marcellus Clay was an important politician. Although this Cassius Clay inherited a large plantation and slaves from his father, he did not believe in slavery. He emancipated, or freed, his slaves and began to speak out against slavery. He became known as an abolitionist, a person who campaigned against slavery in the United States.

In the mid-1800s, the entire nation was divided over the issue of slavery. In general, those who lived in the South supported slavery while those who lived in the North were against it. Since the state of Kentucky is a border state, midway between the North and the South, there were many Kentuckians who supported each position. Cassius Marcellus Clay, the politician, was outspoken in his opposition to slavery — so much so that on several occasions slavery supporters tried to kill him. But Clay refused to be intimidated. When the War between the States broke out, Clay supported the Union and President Abraham Lincoln.

Later, Lincoln rewarded him by naming him the American ambassador to Russia. To many Kentuckians, particularly African Americans, Clay was a hero. That is why Ali's father was named after the abolitionist.

Odessa Clay was of mixed race. One of her great grandfathers was a white man who had a child with a slave, and one of her grandfathers was a white man who married an African American woman. But in her eyes, and in the eyes of American society, Odessa Clay was simply African American.

Like her husband, Odessa grew up in a segregated society in which African Americans did not enjoy the same rights and privileges as white Americans. It was hard for African Americans to find jobs. Odessa's mother worked as a domestic, taking care of the household chores and the young children of a white family. When Odessa became an adolescent, she dropped out of school and also found work as a domestic. Then, when she was sixteen years old, she met twenty-year-old Cassius, whom everyone referred to as Cash. They soon married and settled into their own house in Louisville.

The Clays weren't wealthy, but because Cassius had

little trouble finding work, the family was comfortable, living in a middle-class African American neighborhood in Louisville's West End. From the start both parents doted on their first-born son.

And from the start Cassius junior loved the attention. He was a precocious child who walked and talked at an early age. He never seemed to sit still and had enormous energy, dashing around the house on his tiptoes and talking a mile a minute.

Cassius's upbringing was typical of the times. Odessa was very religious and made sure the family went to church and to Sunday school each week. At the Virginia Street elementary school, Cassius was an average, if somewhat mischievous and talkative, student. Some people believe he may have suffered from dyslexia, a learning disorder that makes it difficult to read. He much preferred art class and working with his hands. He and his younger brother, Rudy, both enjoyed going to work with their father on a painting job. Cash taught them how to mix paint and sometimes allowed his sons to help him lay out and letter the signs.

But apart from the occasional game of touch football, Cassius, like his father, wasn't very interested in sports. It wasn't until he was twelve years old that he was introduced by chance to the sport that would change his life.

Once a year in Louisville, merchants who catered to the community's African American population demonstrated their wares at the Louisville Home Show. The show was held at a local auditorium. To attract crowds the merchants gave children free popcorn and balloons.

Cassius heard about the show and, like any twelve-year-old, decided an afternoon of eating free popcorn and getting balloons would be fun. So he rode his bike to the auditorium, parked outside, and wandered around the show for a few hours with his friends. But when Cassius left the show to go home, his bicycle was gone! It had been stolen.

He broke into tears and stormed back into the auditorium. An adult noticed him crying and asked Cassius what was wrong. He told him that his bike had been stolen and that he wanted to find a policeman. The man knew that a Louisville police officer, Joe Martin, ran a boxing gym in the basement of the auditorium. He told Cassius to go downstairs and report the theft to Martin.

Cassius went down and found Martin. Sniffing and holding back tears, he told Martin that his bike had been stolen and that he wanted to "whup" whomever had taken it.

Martin felt bad. He knew it was very unlikely that the bike would ever be recovered. But he told Cassius, "You better learn how to fight before you start saying you're going to 'whup' someone."

Cassius had never thought about that before, and he looked around the gym. Boys of all sizes and colors were working out, trying to learn how to box. Some were on the floor doing sit-ups and some were skipping rope. Others were standing in front of a mirror, shadowboxing. Another was hitting what is called a speed bag, and another was pounding a large, heavy bag suspended from the ceiling. In the middle of the room was a boxing ring, and two young men wearing protective headgear and gloves were sparring with each other. Martin was moving around the gym, giving all the boys pointers and shouting words of encouragement.

Cassius loved the way the gym looked and felt. He even liked the way it smelled! He had never thought of becoming a boxer before — and despite his threat to "whup" someone, he had never even been in a real fight. He was intrigued by Martin's challenge.

At first glance, the sport of boxing just looks like two people trying to beat each other up. But it is much more than that. Boxing has rules and requires a great deal of skill, discipline, and practice as well as stamina and strategy. Even the toughest street fighter has little chance against a trained boxer.

Boxing is one of the world's oldest sports. For centuries human beings have tried to settle their differences by fighting. But boxing is not a contest motivated by hate; it is one in which the participants test each other's skills. Both the ancient Greeks and Romans competed in a form of boxing, and there are even descriptions of boxing in Homer's epic Greek poem the *Iliad*. In ancient times, boxing matches lasted until one man was too injured to continue.

The modern sport began in England during the 1700s. A man named James Figg opened a boxing school and taught students to throw different punches and block the blows. His students then competed against one another. Before long, spectators came to watch the competitions.

At first there were few rules to boxing. But over time, for reasons of safety, a set of rules slowly evolved.

In the 1860s an Englishman known as the Marquess of Queensberry developed a set of twelve rules that still serves as the basis of the modern sport. The marquess decided that boxers would wear gloves and fight in rounds that would last for two or three minutes, with one minute of rest in between. A boxer who was knocked down had ten seconds to regain his feet. If he could not do so, he was considered knocked out, and the match ended.

Over the next fifty years the rules continued to evolve. Head butts and punches below the belt or to the back of the head were made illegal. Boxers were matched by weight so each fight would be fair. The weight divisions ranged from junior flyweight, for boxers under 108 pounds, to the heavyweight division, for those who weigh above 195 pounds. The number of rounds a fight lasted was limited to fifteen, and in the event no one was knocked out either the referee or a team of judges scored the fight and determined the winner.

Boxing came to the United States early in the

nineteenth century. At first the sport was banned in places because it was considered too violent. But its popularity grew, and soon there were too many boxers, and boxing fans, to stop the sport entirely. By 1920 boxing was a legal sport throughout the United States.

By then, nearly every town and city had one or more gyms where boxing was taught. Boxing matches between professionals sometimes drew thousands of fans. Champions, particularly in the heavyweight division, became rich and famous.

But not everyone who boxed did so for money. Beginning in 1904, boxing became an Olympic sport. Amateur boxers, unlike their professional counterparts, wear protective headgear and larger, padded gloves. In amateur boxing, each match generally lasts only three rounds of two minutes each.

For many years in the United States, African American boxers were not allowed to fight white boxers, and until very recently women were not even allowed to compete in the sport. But in Australia, in 1908, an energetic and powerful African American named Jack Johnson won the world heavyweight title when he defeated white Canadian Tommy Burns.

Such fights between African American and white boxers drew enormous crowds. Soon the ban against African American fighters was dropped in the United States.

Twelve-year-old Cassius Clay knew none of boxing's long history the day he went to the basement of the auditorium in Louisville. All he knew was that his bicycle had been stolen. But when he walked into the gym, the course of his life changed forever.

★ CHAPTER TWO ★

1954–1960

Tomorrow's Champion

Soon after meeting Joe Martin, Cassius Clay began going to the gym and learning how to box. At first he was just one of dozens of young men and boys who worked out there. Martin and his assistant, a man named Fred Stoner, enjoyed their work. They believed boxing gave young men a way to channel their energy. Instead of fighting on the streets or getting in trouble, they came to the gym and fought by the rules in the ring or worked out on the equipment.

Boxing is hard work. If a boxer is going to succeed, he must by disciplined, both physically and emotionally. A person whose emotions run wild will not go far in boxing. Many boys started training at Martin's gym, but only a few stuck it out for long. Most quit after they discovered how hard they had to work — or how painful it was to be punched in the nose.

But young Cassius Clay kept coming back, training six days a week. Martin and Stoner started by teaching him the basics of boxing. He learned how to throw a straight, hard punch known as a jab; a looping punch called a hook; and a punch thrown from below, an uppercut. They taught him to stay on his toes and move around the ring to make himself a difficult target.

Young Cassius paid close attention. He liked the way boxing made him feel about himself. The more he worked out, the stronger and more confident he felt. He even liked sparring with other boxers, although he didn't like getting hit as much as he liked hitting.

After training for just a few weeks, Clay made his debut in the ring. He was only twelve and weighed a mere eighty-nine pounds, yet he defeated his competition. And from then on, there was no going back. In fact, he already knew where he wanted to fight next.

Joe Martin was involved with a local television program called *Tomorrow's Champions*. The show pitted young amateur boxers against one another in exhibition matches. Although the fights weren't considered official, Cassius wanted to be on television.

Three months after he first stepped into the gym, Cassius Clay made his debut television appearance. His opponent was another young man, named Ronnie.

When Cassius stepped in the ring he didn't look anything like "tomorrow's champion." His oversize boxing gloves hung off his arms like two huge pillows, and his face nearly disappeared beneath his protective headgear. When the bell sounded at the start of the first round both boys bolted from their corners, met in the middle of the ring, and starting throwing a flurry of punches. Neither really knew how to box yet, and what little they did know was soon forgotten in the excitement of the moment. Each boy's face stung from the blows, and by the end of the match, each was exhausted.

As in most amateur bouts, the boys had to wait for the judges to select a winner. In amateur boxing, boxers receive points for each punch they throw that hits the target, regardless of how hard it is thrown. A punch that knocks down an opponent, for example, is worth no more than one that is thrown softly.

The judges tallied the score and handed their decision to the referee. The referee then clutched each boy by the hand and an announcer made the call.

"The winner," he said, "by a split decision is" — he hesitated, to make the moment as dramatic as possible. Then he called out — "Cassius Clay!"

Cassius was so excited he nearly jumped out of his boxing trunks. He had won!

Then the announcer stepped toward Cassius with his microphone. After each fight he generally asked the winner a few questions. Often the young boxers were too exhausted and too intimidated by the television camera to say very much. But Cassius Clay was different.

"I'm gonna be the greatest fighter of all times," he blurted out. "The greatest of all times!" The announcer laughed, never suspecting that those words would prove to be prophetic.

Cassius continued to go to the gym six days a week after school for training. He was never late and worked very hard. He listened closely to Martin and Stoner and followed their instructions. He didn't always win his bouts against the other boys, but he didn't let himself get discouraged.

It was when he had been training for about a year that he really began to stand out from the other boxers at the gym. He was simply faster than most boxers his age and had better reflexes. All boxers are told to keep their gloves up and tuck their chins down so they can fend off punches from their opponents. Yet from the start Cassius kept his left hand low, leaving his opponent an opening for a punch to the head.

For most boxers, such a stance is disastrous. But Cassius got away with it almost every time. When his opponent threw a punch at his head, instead of blocking it with hands and arms he simply leaned back or to the side. Instead of landing a solid hit, his opponent's punch would miss or simply strike him with a glancing blow. It was the kind of skill that cannot be taught.

Similarly, his punches were lightning fast. Although he lacked power, for he was still very slender, Cassius rarely had a hard time striking his opponent.

As he continued to train he began to enter tournaments sponsored by the Amateur Athletic Union, the national organization that ran amateur boxing. He also participated in the Golden Gloves annual national tournament.

Joe Martin's wife, Christine, often drove Cassius and other young boxers to tournaments in distant cities like Indianapolis and Toledo. Along the way, the group would have to stop to eat. But at the time, some restaurants did not allow African Americans inside. There were no drive-through windows back then, so Christine Martin would go inside and buy food. Then everyone would eat together in the car.

Cassius never gave Joe Martin any trouble, either in the gym or on his way to a tournament. Christine Martin recalled that while the other boys were cracking jokes and fooling around, Cassius "was sitting and reading his Bible," which, according to her, he carried everywhere.

During his first few years, Cassius had a difficult time in the tournaments. Many of the fighters were more experienced. Losing didn't discourage him, however, and he learned to take something away from each match and to learn from his mistakes. One day while sparring he was knocked out, but he showed up the next day and asked to spar with the same fighter again.

As the months passed, he grew taller, stronger, and faster. By the time he reached high school he was one of the best boxers in Louisville. Followers of amateur boxing began talking about the young Cassius Clay. On October 27, 1957, after defeating an opponent named Donnie Hall on TV, Cassius made it into the newspapers for the first time. A local sportswriter referred to him as "the number-one contender for the light-heavyweight title in the Golden Gloves competition."

But no one talked as much about Cassius Clay as Cassius himself. In the ring and at the gym he was all business, but as soon as his work was over he gave his tongue a workout. He told everybody he was going to be the greatest fighter of all time, and before going into the ring with an opponent he usually told him he was going to "whup" him, as if that person had been the one who had stolen his bicycle. In short, he was a braggart.

Braggarts are usually so self centered that people soon tire of being around them. But Cassius was different. When he bragged it was comical, almost as if he were making fun of himself and knew it. After mouthing off he flashed a ready smile that let everyone know he didn't take himself *too* seriously. When he lost he was a good loser and gave his opponent credit, and when he won he didn't rub it in but found something positive to say about the person he had just beaten. He was so energetic and enthusiastic that no one thought he was obnoxious or stuck up. Instead, people liked being around him because he was always having so much fun.

Cassius kept boxing all throughout high school. Joe Martin later called him "the hardest worker" of any young boxer he had ever trained. Cassius went to bed early, and he never drank alcohol or smoked even as many of his friends experimented with such dangerous substances. He became a familiar figure in Louisville, jogging through the West End, where he sometimes tried to race city buses. After school he worked at a college library, shelving books and sweeping the floors. Then it was off to the gym. He was completely focused on becoming a boxing champion.

But that wasn't entirely good for him. He focused so much on boxing that his grades suffered. When he was in tenth grade he even dropped out of school briefly before his mother convinced him to return. All he wanted to do was box.

And he was getting pretty good at it. Each win gave him more and more confidence, and he loved the attention that came with winning. By the time he was eighteen years old he had fought 108 times, won six state-of-Kentucky Golden Gloves championships, two Golden Gloves national titles, and two Amateur Athletic Union national titles. He had grown into a tall and rangy fighter who now weighed nearly 180 pounds.

Thus far, he had experienced only a few setbacks. In one bout in 1958 he pulled a muscle in his stomach. Joe Martin had the referee stop the fight so Cassius wouldn't be hurt, and he suffered his first defeat in a sanctioned bout. A year later, in an international tournament known as the Pan American Games, he was outpointed by a much-older boxer representing the Marines.

Cassius was anxious to turn professional, but Joe Martin cautioned him against it. He told the young boxer that he should remain an amateur and try to make the Olympic team. A good showing at the Olympics would mean he wouldn't start at the bottom when he turned professional.

Cassius heeded Martin's advice. In 1960, after he won the Amateur Athletic Union national championship, he was asked to attend the trials for the

United States Olympic boxing team. In order to compete in the tournament Cassius had to travel to California.

There was only one problem: he was afraid to fly! He wasn't afraid of other boxers, but the idea of getting into an airplane and flying across the country scared him to death. He had never been on a plane before. It took Joe Martin a long time to convince him to go to California.

By then Cassius was the best-known amateur boxer in the country, but he wasn't known only for his skills in the ring. His mouth was getting him more and more national attention — little of it good.

Everyone in Louisville knew that Cassius liked to talk and brag. They just laughed it off. But boxers from other parts of the country, boxing fans, and sportswriters were put off. Many of them thought he was rude and disrespectful. Some thought he was downright crazy.

When Cassius arrived at the tournament for the Olympic trials, he was his usual overconfident self. At a press conference he was so loud and overbearing that he angered American Olympic officials. A local newspaper wrote that he was ruining a "clean, pure, decent amateur tournament." Fans booed him when he entered the ring for the first time. Afraid that his young boxer would be reprimanded or disqualified for his antics outside the ring, Joe Martin finally told him to watch his mouth.

So Cassius kept his lips sealed and let his fists speak instead. He easily reached the finals in the light-heavyweight division of the trials. He would face opponent Allen Hudson, the light-heavyweight champion of the Army. Hudson wasn't as skilled as Cassius, but he was older and stronger.

In the first round the two fighters appeared evenly matched as they felt each other out. Then, just as Cassius was pulling away after the two fighters had drawn close, Hudson threw a long, looping left hook. Cassius had his arms down and the punch connected with the side of his head.

Boom! He crashed to the canvas. But he was lucky. The punch knocked him down but didn't knock him out. If it had, it may have been the end of his boxing career.

Fortunately, because of the protective headgear worn by all amateur boxers, few experience a knock-out, which can be dangerous. Any hard punch to the head literally causes the brain to bounce back and forth within the skull and bruises it. That is known as a concussion. A knockout is a concussion so severe that it causes unconsciousness.

Fortunately, Cassius wasn't knocked out, but the force of the punch was hard enough to send him to the mat. He bounced back up, and after the referee gave him the mandatory ten-count and made sure he was okay, the fight resumed.

For the rest of the first round and all of the second, the two fighters boxed to a standoff. It is important to understand that in amateur boxing, fighters accumulate points for punches that reach the target even if they are not thrown particularly hard. One boxer may be hit by a number of solid punches yet still win the fight if he or she manages to pepper the opponent with more punches. In some instances, a fighter can be knocked down and still win the bout even though the opponent remained upright the entire fight.

Entering the final round Cassius knew he was probably behind. He had to take the third round to have even a chance to win the bout.

Midway through the round, he got his chance. As

the two fighters came out of a clinch, Cassius threw a hard right-hand punch that connected solidly with Hudson's jaw, staggering the fighter. As Hudson's legs turned to rubber and he struggled to protect himself, Cassius threw a series of scoring punches. Hudson stood almost helpless, holding his arms in front of his face.

Safety is always a major concern in amateur boxing — referees are instructed to stop the match if one boxer can no longer put up a defense. The referee noticed that Hudson wasn't fighting back anymore. He stepped between the two boxers and stopped the fight. Cassius Clay was declared the winner. He was going to the Olympics!

★ CHAPTER THREE ★
1960

Olympic Gold

In the months before the 1960 Olympic Games, scheduled to be held in Rome, Italy, Cassius Clay worked hard. His obvious skill — and his mouth — had gotten the attention of both the American public and sportswriters, who dubbed him the Louisville Lip. *Sports Illustrated* called him "the best American prospect for a gold medal" in boxing, and he was heavily favored to win in the light-heavyweight division. Sportswriters learned that he was always good for a story, and as the Games approached he became one of the best-known athletes on the American team. Cassius brashly predicted that not only would he win a gold medal, but so would many of his teammates.

But as the Olympics drew close, the question of exactly how Cassius would get to Rome went unanswered. He still didn't like to fly, and Joe Martin would be unable to go with him due to an illness in his family. Even as Cassius appeared to be brimming with confidence, part of him was insecure and afraid. Fortunately, Martin was able to convince Cassius to give air travel another try.

The Olympic experience is more than just the time an athlete spends in competition. The larger goal of the Games is to foster understanding between people of different cultures and nationalities. During the Games athletes from all over the world live together in dormitories in the Olympic Village. They eat in the same dining rooms and have the opportunity to get to know one another.

Cassius Clay had never been around so many different people before. But if he was intimidated, he didn't show it. As soon as he arrived in the Village he brashly walked up to strangers, introduced himself, and asked a hundred questions while talking non-stop and flashing a big smile.

It didn't matter if the other athletes understood English or not; it was impossible for them not to like the animated young boxer from Louisville. One teammate joked that if there were an election for mayor of the Olympic Village "he would have won in a walk."

At the same time, however, Cassius didn't forget why he was in Rome. He meant to win and he trained hard, even keeping his teammates awake by shadow-boxing in front of a mirror while they tried to sleep.

Once the Games began, it became clear that Cassius was far more skilled than the competition. Most Olympic boxers had trained in Europe and favored a plodding, straightforward style. But Cassius was different.

For a big man, he was lightning-fast on his feet. As he prowled around the ring he danced on his tip-toes, stepping in to flick a jab in his opponent's face, then deftly dancing out of range before his opponent could respond. It seemed as if Cassius could hit his opponent at will and almost avoid being hit himself altogether.

He dispatched his first three opponents with ease, earning the right to box for the gold medal against the Polish champion, Zbigniew "Ziggy" Pietrzykowski. But unlike his previous opponents, Pietrzykowski would prove to be a challenge.

The Polish fighter was left handed, and Cassius had very little experience fighting a southpaw. Most boxers are right handed and stand with their body turned slightly so that their left shoulder is in front. But Pietrzykowski stood the opposite way. That made it awkward for Cassius to dance in and out the way he was accustomed to.

The match was broadcast back to the United States. All of Louisville and most of the country gathered around television sets to see if Cassius could back up his talk with a gold medal.

At first, he was completely confused by Pietrzykowski. Each time he danced in to throw a punch, Pietrzykowski beat him to it, pounding Cassius in the face. During one exchange Cassius took such a beating that he even closed his eyes and winced before dancing back out of range. All his speed and fancy footwork were going to waste. When the bell rang to signal the end of round one, it was obvious that Cassius was losing.

Round two started off the way round one had ended, with Cassius being pounded by his opponent. It was beginning to appear as if Cassius would have to settle for a silver medal.

Then, quick as a wink, he changed his style.

Instead of trying to dance and jab, Cassius decided to stand toe to toe with the Polish fighter. It was a risky strategy, for it put him within range of the powerful puncher. But at the same time it allowed Cassius to take aim himself.

All of a sudden, Cassius's punches started finding their mark. He discovered he could hit his opponent — and hit him hard. Near the end of the round he landed four solid right jabs in a row, leaving Pietrzykowski stunned.

Now Cassius had a chance. He realized he might still be behind in the fight, but at least he had put himself in position to win.

When the bell rang to start the third round, Cassius noticed that his opponent was slower and more cautious than before. Those big punches at the end of the second round were still having an effect. If the Polish boxer had thought to coast through the final round and emerge with a win, he soon found he was sadly mistaken.

Cassius danced in and out, throwing a wide variety of punches. He pounded the Polish fighter, who quickly became defenseless under the onslaught. Soon there was blood dripping from the other man's face, and a moment later, the referee stopped the fight. Cassius Clay was an Olympic champion!

He could hardly contain his excitement at the ceremony when he received his medal. As he left the ring, he let it all out, yelling to everyone, "I told you! I did it! I am the greatest!" That night Cassius was so proud of his medal he slept with it around his neck. He wore it every day for weeks.

Boxing observers were impressed. Not only had he shown a great deal of ability, but he also appeared able to sense a weakness in his opponent and to change his style in the middle of a fight. That was a skill that couldn't be taught and one that would serve him well as a professional. And now that Cassius was a gold-medal winner, his career as a professional boxer was drawing closer.

When Cassius returned to the United States, Joe Martin met him in New York to show him the city and discuss his future. Martin was now a part of a group of investors who were interested in backing Cassius in a professional career.

But first, Cassius got to enjoy his new status as a celebrity. He walked all over New York and took in the sights while wearing his Olympic jacket and his gold medal. Everywhere he went, he was greeted by calls of "Welcome home, champ!" He met former boxing champion Sugar Ray Robinson and stayed in a fancy hotel, where he ate four steaks every day and had a room next to the Prince of Wales.

But the biggest celebration came when he returned home to Louisville. His plane was met by a police motorcade that brought Cassius to his old school, Central High. At a reception, the school gave its most famous recent graduate his own letter jacket.

For once, Cassius was almost speechless. "I appreciate this," he finally blurted out. "Thank you very much."

Soon Cassius had to decide what the next step in his life would be. A wealthy heir to a tobacco fortune and friend of Joe Martin, Bill Reynolds, believed that Cassius could become the heavyweight champion of the world. He wanted to sponsor Cassius's professional career and offered Cassius a ten-thousand-dollar bonus plus a salary for ten years to help him achieve that goal. Of course, in the event that Cassius became successful and earned a great deal of money, Reynolds would get a substantial percentage of his earnings.

Reynolds met with Cassius, his parents, and their attorney and presented his proposal. Everyone but Cassius senior was satisfied with the arrangement.

If Cassius signed with Reynolds, Joe Martin, policeman, would still serve as Cassius's trainer. But Cassius senior had been in some minor trouble with the law and didn't trust the police. Besides, other figures much more experienced in pro boxing, such as the trainer Cus D'Amato and boxer Archie Moore, were clamoring for the right to train and represent his son. In the end, the Clays turned the deal down.

At length, however, they accepted a proposal from another Louisville businessman, Bill Faversham. He formed the Louisville Sponsoring Group, a syndicate of eleven wealthy businessmen. They gave Cassius a ten-thousand-dollar bonus, and a two-hundred-dollar-a-month salary for the next two years, and they agreed to absorb all training costs and expenses. In exchange they would receive half of all the money Cassius Clay earned.

Cassius Clay was now a professional boxer. A great journey was about to begin.

⋆ CHAPTER FOUR ⋆
1960–1963

The Louisville Lip

Before becoming a professional boxer, Cassius Clay rarely spoke about matters of race. During the Olympics, a Russian journalist asked him how it felt to win a gold medal for a nation where he "couldn't eat at the same table as a white man." Clay was taken aback and told him, "We got qualified people working on that and I'm not worried about the outcome. The U.S.A. is still the greatest country in the world."

But that did not mean that Clay was not aware of the racial problems that existed in America. African Americans were still openly discriminated against. In some localities it was against the law for African Americans and whites to share the same bathrooms or water fountains or to sit at the same lunch counters. African Americans suspected of breaking segregation laws were sometimes beaten up by police. Other

times they were kidnapped by mobs and killed —
this was known as lynching. It was difficult for many
African Americans, no matter how qualified, to get
any job but the most menial.

When Cassius Clay was growing up, Louisville was
still very much a segregated city, and African Americans weren't welcome in certain neighborhoods,
stores, restaurants, and hotels except as workers.
Clay's mother cleaned the homes of white families,
and Cassius senior often told his son how hard life
was for African Americans and pointed out the prej-
udices African Americans faced.

Although few people knew it, Clay had already
started taking a serious look at what it meant to be
an African American. While he was in high school
he even wrote a paper on an obscure group known
as the Nation of Islam, a religious organization that
preached separatism between the races. The paper
upset his teacher so much she wanted to fail him,
only to have the principal overrule her.

Yet up to this point in his young life, Clay had kept
his thoughts on such serious issues to himself. His
fame as a boxer had helped shield him from the
worst aspects of prejudice. But as he became a man,

Cassius Clay began to think for himself and to see the world in a new light.

For now he was still focused on becoming a champion. A short time after he signed his contract with the Louisville Sponsoring Group, he fought his first pro fight in Fayetteville, West Virginia, against Tunney Hunsaker.

Although Hunsaker had more professional experience than Clay, he couldn't match Clay's overall experience, gained from hundreds of amateur bouts. Clay adapted easily to boxing without protective headgear and wasn't bothered by fighting an additional minute in each round. Before six thousand fans, Clay earned a six-round decision and won a two-thousand-dollar purse.

Hunsaker was impressed and later told people that he believed Clay "would be heavyweight champion of the world someday." But Clay's backers had expected a knockout and were disappointed. Clay was still fighting as he had as an amateur, scoring by peppering his opponent with punches and winning on points. But in pro boxing the power of a punch, particularly those thrown at the head, is valued by judges, and no professional fighter succeeds for very long without demonstrating that he or she has the power to knock out an opponent. Clay's sponsors wanted to make certain that the young professional developed a professional style. They decided to send Clay to train with veteran boxer Archie Moore.

Moore was forty-seven years old in November 1960, when Clay arrived at the training camp known as the Salt Mine. Moore had been boxing as a professional since 1936, and in his long career he had seen it all. The Louisville Sponsorsing Group hoped that Moore could turn Clay into a powerful and polished pro.

Moore was impressed with Clay, but the young boxer grated against the discipline Moore demanded from his student. As the youngest boxer in the camp, Clay was expected to do chores like washing the dishes. Clay thought that was a waste of his time. Although Moore and Clay respected each other, they simply didn't agree about training methods. Clay stayed with Moore for just over a month, then left.

Fortunately, he was sent to Miami to work with trainer Angelo Dundee at his famous Fifth Street Gym. Dundee immediately recognized that Clay's speed, reflexes, and personality made him special.

Like nearly everyone else who met Clay, Dundee couldn't help but like the talkative young man. Instead of trying to change his style, Dundee decided he would simply take advantage of the gifts Clay already had.

He planned to bring Clay along slowly, balancing time spent training in the gym with a series of fights against lesser opponents to build his confidence. Over the next four months Clay fought four times. He either knocked out his opponent or hurt him badly enough that the fight was stopped, causing what is known as a technical knockout, or TKO.

Then Clay made a television appearance with a professional wrestler known as Gorgeous George. The popular wrestler talked even more than Clay did, taunting his opponents and touting his own ability. Half the fans loved him and wanted to see him win, while the others hated him and hoped to see him lose. As a result he was the biggest drawing card in the sport.

Clay was intrigued and realized he could draw the same kind of attention. He began talking even more and before every fight started predicting the round in which he would knock out his opponent. That got everyone's attention. No boxer had ever done that before, at least not very accurately.

Late in 1961, Clay made three appearances on national television fighting on a program known as the *Cavalcade of Sports*. In his third appearance, facing a fighter named Willi Besmanoff, Clay unveiled his new approach. He predicted that he would knock out Besmanoff in the seventh round and boasted, "I'm ready for the top contender."

When the fight began Clay put on a show that few fans ever forgot. He danced and jabbed and talked and ducked his way through the first six rounds, toying with his opponent. But in the seventh round he turned it all up a notch and flattened Besmanoff just as he had predicted. After the fight he chortled before the camera, saying, "I am the greatest, I am the greatest!"

Fans hardly knew what to think. Some thought he was crazy. They were accustomed to boxers, particularly African American boxers, who behaved much more respectfully. Clay's immense confidence and brash way of speaking got a great deal of attention. As with Gorgeous George, some fans loved it and others hated it. But everyone was interested in his next fight.

Over the following year Clay kept fighting and talking and drawing more attention to himself. He also kept winning, running his record to 13–0. Dundee decided he was ready for his first big fight. Clay's opponent would be none other than Archie Moore.

Although Moore had fought more than two hundred bouts, it was finally becoming clear that his days as a fighter were drawing to a close. But Moore was popular and remained a skilled boxer. Dundee knew a Clay-Moore matchup would cause a stir. If Clay defeated a boxer like Moore, he would suddenly be considered a true contender for the heavyweight title.

The fight, scheduled for October 23, 1962, was a promoter's dream. During a series of press conferences the two boxers drummed up public interest in the bout. The contrast between Clay and Moore was dramatic. Clay was lean and brash and had his whole future ahead of him. Moore, on the other hand, was heavy and graying and represented boxing's past. The two bantered back and forth easily, trading mostly good-natured insults. Moore claimed he had developed a new punch for Clay that he called the lip-buttoner, while Clay made his feelings clear in a poem that ended, "When you come to the fight don't block the aisle or door / 'Cause y'all going home after round four."

The bout drew as much attention as a championship fight. Hundreds of thousands of boxing fans jammed theaters to watch the fight on closed-circuit TV. They weren't disappointed. Clay made his prediction come true. In the fourth round Moore went down in a flurry of punches. A few moments after he got back up, the fight was stopped. Clay had defeated his former trainer with a TKO.

The victory vaulted Clay into the top ten of the heavyweight division. He was now considered a contender for the heavyweight title then currently held by Floyd Patterson.

Angelo Dundee knew that Clay still had some growing to do before he fought for the title and remained patient with the young star. He wanted Clay to wait several years and gain more experience. Then, if he kept progressing, he would be prepared to fight for the title. But Clay's growth and development weren't confined to the boxing ring.

Fame gave Clay confidence and exposed him to people and ideas that he otherwise may never have known. His education as a human being was taking place at the same fast pace as his education as a boxer.

Although Clay had been raised as a Christian by his mother, recent experiences had caused him to question many of his beliefs. He began to suspect that many white people he interacted with were not sincere. He wondered if they would treat him the same were he not a famous boxer, a notion he found troubling. The religious philosophy of the Nation of Islam, popularly known in the press as "the Black Muslims," seemed to provide some answers to the questions Clay was wrestling with. In 1962, he began to take a serious look at the Nation.

The Nation of Islam was an African American form of the Islamic religion. The followers of Islam believe in the teachings of the prophet Muhammad, which are written in a book called the Koran or Qur'an. Considered one of the world's great religions, Islam is practiced by millions of people in many countries.

The Nation of Islam, however, is a distinct form of Islam that has been particularly appealing to African

Americans. It began in the 1930s when two African American men, Wallace Fard and Elijah Poole, claimed to receive revelations as prophets of Islam and created the new religion. Elijah Poole began using the name Elijah Muhammad and became the leader of the Nation. The founders adopted portions of orthodox Islamic teachings but added several new elements that were particularly attractive to African Americans, who suffered from discrimination in American society. While the religion taught African Americans to be self-reliant and to live moral lives free of drugs and alcohol, it also viewed white people as "devils" responsible for oppressing the African race. The Nation of Islam preached that the races should be separate and that white people could not be trusted. While some followers found that this philosophy provided some answers in their lives, many Americans, both black and white, believed the Nation of Islam was a hate-based group that preached racism.

In the early 1960s the civil-rights movement, led by people such as the Reverend Martin Luther King Jr., called for equality for African Americans and pushed for political changes to guarantee equal rights for all. As the civil-rights movement began to gain support in the United States, so too did the Nation of Islam. A dynamic speaker named Malcolm X brought new attention to the cause with his fiery speeches.

Soon after becoming a professional boxer, Cassius Clay heard Malcolm X speak. He began reading Nation of Islam publications. Much of what he learned made sense to him. After all, even though he was a famous boxer he was still working for a group of white men, the Louisville Sponsoring Group, and they were still taking half of all the money he earned. That didn't seem right or fair. Beginning in 1962, twenty-year-old Cassius Clay began to study the teachings of the Nation of Islam.

Likewise, the Nation began to try to convert Clay from Christianity. Clay was becoming one of the most famous African Americans in the country. His conversion was certain to attract attention and help the Nation spread its message.

At the time, few American sports heroes ever advocated racial, religious, or political views. But as Cassius Clay began to be influenced by the Nation of Islam, he began to speak out, saying that he believed it was natural for African Americans to be with

43

their "own kind" and giving his support to the civil-rights movement. Many Americans, particularly those who didn't recognize the need for change, began to resent Clay for his very public opinions.

Initially, his outspokenness seemed to have little effect on his boxing career. After a tough victory over Doug Jones in New York in June 1963, Clay went to England to face the British boxer Henry Cooper.

Clay was shocked when he arrived in London and discovered that everybody already knew who he was. He knew he was becoming famous in the United States, but he had no idea his popularity had already reached Europe. The British press lavished him with attention even though they considered him foolish for predicting a fifth-round knockout.

Few observers expected Clay to have much trouble with Cooper, who was known for only one punch, a left hook. For the first few rounds of the fight Clay appeared in complete control. He was much faster than Cooper and seemed to be toying with the boxer, hitting him at will and then dancing around the ring, showing off his dazzling footwork. By the fourth round Cooper's face was swollen and stained with his own blood. A raucous crowd began calling for the fight to be stopped.

But just before the end of the fourth round, Cooper finally executed his powerful hook, catching Clay flush on the jaw. Clay fell back into the ropes and then lurched face forward onto the canvas.

The crowd suddenly roared for Cooper. It appeared that he had knocked Clay out!

As the referee counted to ten, Clay managed to stand. But he was clearly hurt. Just when Cooper was poised to resume his attack, the bell rang, signaling the end of the round.

Clay retreated to his corner and slumped into his seat, barely conscious. Unless he recovered quickly, his opponent was nearly certain to put him back on the canvas in the fifth round.

Then Angelo Dundee noticed a small tear in the seam of Clay's glove. Boxers generally aren't allowed to fight with damaged equipment. Just as the fifth round was scheduled to begin he brought the glove to the referee's attention.

While the referee examined the glove, Clay received some extra time to clear his head. After a minute the referee ruled that Clay could continue to fight with the glove. By then, Clay had recovered from the near knockout.

That was the only break Clay needed. As the bell sounded to begin again, Clay roared out to the center of the ring and put on a dazzling display. It was the fifth round, after all — time for him to make his prediction come true.

Observers had never seen a fighter look so fast, strong, and powerful. Clay unleashed a furious attack. Each time one of his punches found Cooper's face, blood splattered all over the ring. In a matter of seconds Cooper's face was cut to ribbons and he could barely see. The referee stepped in and stopped the fight.

Afterwards Clay admitted, "Cooper is a real fighter." But he was already looking ahead. He started screaming and yelling, "I'm the greatest. Not only do I knock them out, I pick the round. I am the prettiest, most superior scientific boxer in the ring today."

Then he started screaming about fighting another man, Sonny Liston. Several months before Liston had scored a first-round knockout against Floyd Patterson to win the world heavyweight championship. "I don't need Sonny —" boasted Clay, "Sonny needs me!"

Many sportswriters in the crowd shook their heads with disbelief. Sonny Liston had lost only once, in the early stages of his career. Since then he had been unstoppable. He was a huge man with an enormous punch and a former convict with a well-deserved reputation as one of the most dangerous fighters in boxing history. What was Cassius Clay doing, they wondered, trying to get a boxer like Sonny Liston all worked up?

The world would soon find out.

★ CHAPTER FIVE ★

1964

Champion!

In 1963, many observers thought Sonny Liston was the greatest boxer in history. He was certainly the most feared.

Liston had a rough upbringing and had been arrested many times, even going to prison for armed robbery and for attacking a police officer. There were rumors that he was connected to organized crime and had been an "enforcer" for mobsters, beating people up on command.

But he was also a tremendous boxer, tall and strong, with long arms that made it hard for other boxers to get at him. He enjoyed his unsavory reputation. Most opponents were so intimidated by Liston that they were defeated before they even stepped into the ring.

Liston was in no hurry to fight Clay. He first wanted to fight a lucrative rematch against Patterson and then cash in on his title with some easy fights.

Neither Angelo Dundee nor the Louisville Sponsoring Group thought Clay was close to being ready for Liston. After all, he was only twenty-one and had fought fewer than twenty professional fights. He had never had to fight for more than ten rounds. They wanted him to get several more years of experience.

But Cassius Clay was impatient. He wanted to fight Liston now, and he had a plan to make it a reality. He decided to get Liston so angry that he would have to give him a fight.

A month after Clay's victory over Cooper, Liston was scheduled to fight his rematch with Patterson. Clay began stalking Liston, trying to provoke him and get boxing fans excited about seeing the two men meet in the ring.

The fight between Liston and Patterson was scheduled to take place in Las Vegas. Clay was invited to attend and to be introduced to the crowd before the fight. He arrived in Las Vegas a few days before the bout and followed Liston into a casino, then watched as he gambled.

Liston ignored him until Clay got started. He began screaming at Liston, calling him a "big, ugly bear." The crowd at the casino watched as Liston got angrier and angrier.

Finally Liston walked over to Clay and told him he was going to "pull that big tongue out" of his mouth. For a moment it looked as if Liston was going to hit Clay; the young boxer wisely withdrew. But he now had Liston's attention.

A few nights later Liston demolished Patterson in one round with a devastating attack that left boxing fans breathless. Liston seemed unbeatable.

It was a big night for the boxer. But moments after the fight Clay jumped into the ring, grabbed the microphone, and stole all of Liston's thunder. "Liston is a tramp," he said. "I'm the champ. I want that big, ugly bear. I'm tired of talking. If I can't whip that bum, I'll leave the country."

Liston seethed with anger. After the fight he was all but ignored. Everyone in boxing was talking about Clay.

Over the next few months Clay continued to provoke Liston, once even showing up on his front lawn at two in the morning and challenging the champion. In November 1963 Clay finally got his wish. Liston was so eager to shut him up that he agreed to fight Clay for the heavyweight title. The match would take place in February 1964 in Miami, Florida.

Most experienced boxing observers just shook their heads. They thought Clay didn't stand a chance and that behind all his talk he was scared to death. In a poll of forty-six boxing writers from around the country, forty-three predicted a Liston victory, most by an early knockout.

In the days before the fight Clay never shut up. He predicted a victory in eight rounds and even wrote a long, humorous poem about it, saying the fight would end in "a total eclipse of the Sonny." He kept referring to Liston as a "bear" and called him "ugly" and an "old man." As the fight approached many boxing fans thought Clay was crazy.

He was crazy — but he was crazy like a fox. Although he was cautious of the champion, all his bold talk was designed to make Liston think that perhaps Clay *was* crazy, that he was capable of doing anything in the ring. Clay was trying to intimidate Liston.

Interest in the fight was enormous. All 8,300 seats at the Miami Beach Convention Center were sold out and nearly one million fans bought tickets to watch the fight on closed-circuit television in theaters around the world. If nothing else, Clay's talk guaranteed the match would be lucrative for both fighters.

Outwardly Liston appeared to remain calm, promising to shut Clay up for good. But at the weigh-in before the fight Clay went over the top. He wore a jacket that said "Bear Huntin'" on the back. As one of his supporters chanted, "Float like a butterfly, sting like a bee," and "Rumble, young man, rumble," Clay started screaming, "I can beat you anytime, chump. Someone's gonna die tonight!" He acted so crazy that the local boxing commission fined him $2,500. He entered the fight a 7–1 underdog.

When the bell rang to start the fight, Clay danced around the ring at a frenetic pace, throwing the occasional jab at Liston and then dancing away. To many it looked as if he was afraid of the champion.

In the second round, however, he stood toe to toe with the bigger boxer and the two exchanged a series of blows. Although Clay lost the round, it gave him confidence. He had taken some heavy punches and hadn't been hurt.

He danced through the third and fourth rounds and his left jab began to find Liston's face. At the end of the fourth round, although Clay's eye was beginning to swell, the skin around both of Liston's eyes was puffy and his face was cut.

In round five Clay kept pawing at his own eyes. When the round ended, he returned to his corner and told Dundee that there was something in them. He couldn't see and he wanted to quit the bout.

The trainer couldn't believe his ears. He assumed that whatever had been applied to Liston's cut had somehow gotten in Clay's eyes. He flushed them with water and told him, "This is for the heavyweight championship. No one walks away from that! Get in there and run until your eyes clear." Clay reluctantly agreed.

He kept out of range in round five, blinking repeatedly, and by the start of round six his vision cleared. Then Clay started dancing again. It was clear to everyone that he was much faster than Liston, who was having trouble hitting the moving target. Meanwhile Clay was beginning to hit Liston at will.

The fight still appeared a long way from being over. But as Liston slumped on his stool after round six, he suddenly spit out his mouthpiece. It took only a moment for the crowd to realize what that meant. Sonny Liston had quit!

The referee came over to Clay, raised his arm over his head, and declared him champion of the world. The arena erupted and words flowed from Clay's mouth like lava from a volcano. "I am the greatest," he screamed. "I'm king of the world! I shook up the world! I'm a bad man! I'm the prettiest thing that ever lived!"

After the fight Liston claimed that he had hurt his shoulder and was unable to continue. But many thought he had simply given up when he realized he was losing.

Cassius Clay was the heavyweight champion of the world — but not for long.

★ CHAPTER SIX ★

1964–1965

A Member of the Nation

In the weeks and months before the fight, there had been rumors that Clay was becoming closer to joining the Nation of Islam. In fact, for much of the last two or three years he had occasionally attended meetings. Sportswriters had ignored the stories, but now that Clay was a world champion every aspect of his life was subject to examination.

At a press conference the morning after the fight, one writer asked Clay directly, "Are you a Black Muslim?"

Clay didn't back down. He politely corrected the questioner, telling him that "Black Muslim" was a phrase only the press used to describe members of the Nation of Islam. He admitted that he was a member and explained the basic teachings of the group, saying, "I believe in the religion of Islam, which means I believe there is no God but Allah. . . . I know where I am going and I know the truth and I don't have to be what you want me to be."

Then he said that he was renouncing the name Clay, which he described as a "slave name." Elijah Muhammad would soon be giving him a new name. Until then he wanted to be called Cassius X.

The press was stunned by the announcement. Before the Liston fight they had enjoyed the young boxer, laughing at his antics while appreciating his skills in the ring. Now he was the heavyweight champion and wanted to be taken seriously. They were not accustomed to African Americans who thought for themselves, and many became angry.

A week later, on March 6, 1964, Cassius X, formerly Cassius Marcellus Clay, became Muhammad Ali. Almost overnight fans of Clay turned against Ali. Most sportswriters and others refused to call him by his new name. The Black Muslims were considered dangerous, and many thought they were out to destroy Ali.

But Ali was secure with his decision. All he wanted to do was continue his boxing career and practice his religion just like any other American. But over time he would find both increasingly difficult. Soon after he made his announcement he was denounced by a host of prominent Americans, from former heavy-weight champion Joe Louis to Martin Luther King. The World Boxing Association even tried to strip Ali of his title on a technicality.

A short time later Ali traveled to Africa, where he was welcomed as the first Muslim to win a boxing world championship. Word of his victory over Liston had traveled quickly and Ali was greeted as a hero everywhere he went. People of color admired him for standing up for his beliefs and for being proud of his race.

When he returned to the United States he immediately began training for a rematch with Liston, scheduled for November 16, 1964, in Boston. In the minds of many the question of who was the better fighter was still unanswered. The rematch would determine that.

But as the fight approached, Ali found himself in a unique position. He had been the sentimental favorite in the first fight. Now, as champion, public sentiment shifted toward Liston.

Just three days before the fight, Ali was hospitalized

with a hernia and the fight was postponed. While he recovered the Nation of Islam was rocked by infighting and controversy. Prominent Nation leader Malcolm X was assassinated. Two days later the Nation's main office in New York was firebombed. Fearing violence, the Boston promoter canceled the fight between Ali and Liston.

At length, another fight was scheduled for May 25, 1965, in Lewiston, Maine. Both Liston and Ali trained hard. Most observers expected a long, tough match.

When the bell rang at the start of the fight, Ali ran straight across the ring, fired a punch at Liston's face, and then danced away as Liston plodded toward the champion. Ali kept dancing, a big smile on his face, and fired a second punch before dancing away again.

With each blow Liston seemed to get angrier. He began stalking Ali, trying to cut off the ring to keep him from dancing away. He hoped to pin him against the ropes.

Finally, Liston appeared to have Ali cornered. He threw a jab that left him slightly off balance. Ali slipped his head to the side to avoid the punch and then flicked out a quick right hand.

Twelve-year-old Cassius Marcellus Clay Jr. before his amateur debut in 1954.

Olympic gold medal winner Cassius Clay is flanked by two other gold medal winners at the 1960 Olympics in Rome, Italy.

Muhammad Ali, formerly Cassius Clay, stands with Malcolm X of the Nation of Islam on March 19, 1964.

Muhammad Ali delivers the "phantom punch" that sends Sonny
Liston to the mat in Lewiston, Maine, on May 25, 1965.

Muhammad Ali, shown here with civil rights leader Martin Luther King Jr., was an outspoken supporter of the movement.

Perspiration flies from George Foreman's face after Muhammad
Ali connects with a right-hand punch in Zaire on October 30, 1974.

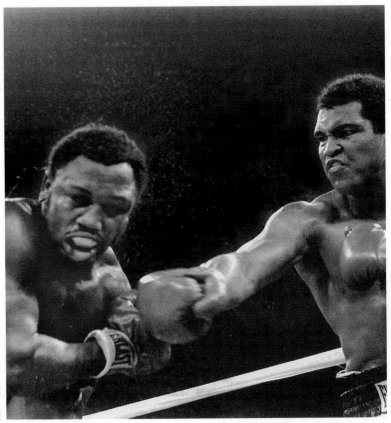

The October 1, 1975, Thrilla-in-Manila match—Muhammad Ali
scores a direct hit on Joe Frazier in the fourteenth round.

The gentle giant receives a hug from a six-year-old girl in Detroit in 2002.

Most people watching the fight never saw the punch. But it knocked Liston to the ground.

The crowd roared. The first round had hardly started and Liston was down!

Instead of retreating to his corner, Ali stood over Liston, yelling, "Get up, get up, you bum, get up!" Referee Jersey Joe Walcott, a former champion, tried to get Ali to back off. When he finally did, Liston stood. Walcott, who had become so flustered that he hadn't bothered to start a ten-count, prepared to let the fight continue.

Then a journalist at the ringside got Walcott's attention and told him, "Liston was down for seventeen seconds. The fight is over." Walcott agreed and raised Ali's arm in triumph.

The crowd started to *boo*. They hadn't seen the punch and thought the fight was fixed — they assumed it had been arranged beforehand that Liston would pretend to be knocked out. Fixing a fight is illegal, but people do it anyway because they can make a lot of money by betting on the person they know will win.

To this day the punch is known as the phantom

punch. Although film of the fight clearly shows that Ali threw a punch, it was so short and quick it seems hard to believe it could have knocked Liston down, much less have knocked him out. But it did. Later Liston admitted that although the punch hadn't hurt him badly, after he was knocked down he was simply afraid to get back up.

Muhammad Ali had won his first bout.

✯ CHAPTER SEVEN ✯

1965–1967

Standing Up

Despite the controversy over his fight with Liston, Muhammad Ali was now the undisputed heavy-weight champion of the world. But that didn't make him any more popular. Instead, he was the object of increasing criticism.

Ali offended former champion Floyd Patterson, for one. After signing up to fight Ali on November 22, 1965, Patterson told a magazine that, "I have nothing but contempt for the Black Muslims and that for which they stand. The image of a Black Muslim as the world heavyweight champion disgraces the sport and the nation. Cassius Clay must be beaten and the Black Muslim scourge removed from boxing."

Patterson's words hurt Ali. He had once looked up to the former champion, but now he was offended by the way Patterson attacked his religion and refused to call him by his new name. Ali, in fact, had never fully embraced the Nation's hatred for whites. He found much more to agree with in their message of self-reliance.

Nevertheless, Ali was angry, and as the fight approached the war of words between the two boxers became more heated. Ali lashed back, calling Patterson a "deaf, dumb Negro who needs a spanking. I plan on punishing him for the things he said."

When the fight began, that's exactly what happened. In the first round Ali didn't even throw a punch. He danced in and out and around the entire round as Patterson, looking old and slow, tried to land a punch. He couldn't.

In round two Ali began his promised punishment. For the rest of the fight he would bob in, pound away for a moment, then step back just as it looked like Patterson was about to fall. Ali kept it up for twelve long rounds, taking Patterson to the brink of a knockout and then backing off over and over again. It was like watching a cat toy with a mouse. Even Angelo Dundee pleaded with him to stop acting so cruel and to end the fight.

The referee finally stopped it in round twelve. Afterwards, Ali was heavily criticized for his brutality. One sportswriter compared him to a "little boy pulling the wings off a butterfly." But Ali was unapologetic. Patterson had insulted his religion.

At the same time that Ali faced this heavy criticism, boxing observers were beginning to realize that Ali just might be, as he said of himself, "the greatest of all times." Clearly, no heavyweight had ever been so fast or light on his feet, and he had demonstrated that when he wanted to he could throw punches with surprising power. Moreover, Ali seemed capable of fighting any way he wanted, any time he wanted. But there was trouble waiting outside the ring.

In the 1960s the United States was at war with Vietnam, a nation that had been torn apart by internal conflict. The Communist forces of the north, the Vietcong, were trying to take over the south. The United States didn't want Communism to spread and decided to help defend South Vietnam. At first only a few hundred, and then a few thousand, soldiers were involved. But by 1964 the war had grown, and despite widespread opposition at home, the United States began sending hundreds of thousands of troops to Vietnam.

The American soldiers did the best they could.

But the Vietcong were defending their home. They believed in their cause, making them hard to defeat. As time went on more and more American soldiers were killed, while the end of the war didn't seem any closer. Meanwhile, opposition to the war in the United States increased.

In 1960, as required by law, Ali had registered for the military draft. In 1964 he had been tested for military service and was turned down when he failed an IQ, or intelligence quotient, test, likely because of his dyslexia. Still, he was embarrassed. But in 1966, in need of more troops, the United States lowered the IQ standard. Suddenly Muhammad Ali was eligible to be drafted.

Ali didn't want to join the military. For one, he thought he was being singled out because he was famous. He also didn't want to suspend his boxing career. At the same time, he felt that it was against his religion to fight in a war. When he was informed that his draft status had been upgraded, a reporter asked him how he felt about the Vietnam War.

"I ain't got no quarrel with them Vietcong," he replied, and soon applied for conscientious-objector status, a designation given to those who could prove that it was against their moral or religious beliefs to fight in war. According to Islam, it is immoral to fight in any war unless it is in defense of the religion.

His words and approach were controversial. All over the country sportswriters and politicians criticized Ali for being unpatriotic. They also accused him of being a coward, of trying to use his religion to dodge the draft. Many of them questioned his sincerity or thought the Nation of Islam was telling him what to do.

While the military considered his application, Ali continued fighting. He was at his peak, in perfect condition, and his contract with the Louisville Sponsoring Group had expired, putting him in control of his own career. Between March and September of 1966 he took his show on the road, fighting four times — once in Canada, twice in England, and once in Germany — and winning easily each time. In part, he wanted the rest of the world to see him, but at the same time he was receiving an increasingly hostile reception in the United States. His stance against the war had turned even more people against him and made it difficult for him to receive permission to box in the United States.

But not everyone considered him an enemy. In fact, his stance made him a hero to those who thought the United States was wrong to be in Vietnam in the first place. Public support for the war was starting to erode as more and more of the country's young men were killed or returned to the United States wounded. The United States wasn't winning, and it was becoming apparent that many Vietnamese people, even in the anti-Communist south, didn't want American troops in their country.

Almost by accident — for he was one of the first famous Americans to speak out against the war — Muhammad Ali became a symbol of the opposition to the Vietnam War. The civil-rights movement turned against the war as well, for while many white Americans could avoid military service through college deferments, segregation and discrimination prevented most African Americans from doing the same. Ali thus became a symbol of the civil-rights movement as well. And he didn't try to hide from his words but continued to voice his opposition.

In August 1966 Ali appeared at a hearing to consider his application as a conscientious objector. In both a written statement and in an interview, Ali calmly and logically defended his application according to the teachings of Islam. To the surprise of many, the hearing officer accepted his application as genuine and recommended that he be given conscientious-objector status.

Had Muhammad Ali not been so famous and controversial, no one would have challenged his designation as a conscientious objector. But Ali's draft board overruled the hearing officer and rejected the claim. They scheduled his induction into the Army for April 28, 1967.

Ali was upset, but he didn't allow it to affect his performance in the ring. Over the next six months he fought and won three more times.

The American military did not expect Ali to serve like other soldiers. They assured him that he would be assigned to Special Services, a wing of the Army that helps improve morale in the troops. In World War II, hundreds of major-league baseball players had been assigned to Special Services and spent most of that war playing baseball exhibitions to entertain the troops. Heavyweight champion Joe Louis had also served in Special Services, fighting in exhibitions and helping to sell war bonds to support the war effort. Ali was assured that he would not have to pick up a gun or enter combat. All he would have to do would be to fight in exhibitions for a few years and then resume his boxing career.

But Ali rejected the offer. He was sincere in his opposition to the war. In early April 1967 he told a magazine, "Why should I put on a uniform and go ten thousand miles from home and drop bombs and bullets on brown people while so-called Negro people in Louisville are treated like dogs?"

Ali showed up for his induction on April 28. When an induction officer called out the name Cassius Marcellus Clay, still his legal name at the time, Ali refused to step forward. A little over a week later he was formally charged with refusing induction, a criminal charge that carried as much as a five-year prison sentence and a heavy fine.

Although Ali was worried about the charge, his conscience was clear. He had remained true to himself. As he said later, "All I did was stand up for what I believed in."

For that, however, he would pay a heavy price.

⋆ CHAPTER EIGHT ⋆

1967–1970

Exile

The boxing world didn't wait for the outcome of the trial before punishing Ali. The World Boxing Association stripped him of his championship belt and ruled that the heavyweight title was vacant. They announced plans to hold a tournament among the top heavyweight contenders to name a new champion. Muhammad Ali would not be allowed to participate.

Over the next few months Ali faced enormous pressure to back down. After all, his stance was costing him his career. A group of prominent African American athletes such as basketball star Bill Russell and football running back Jim Brown even met with Ali to give him advice. Prior to the meeting most believed that Ali had been manipulated by the Nation of Islam into making a stand. But after talking with Ali, the other athletes came away impressed with his sincerity and conviction. "He has something very few people I know possess," said Russell. "He has an absolute and sincere faith."

That didn't matter to the Army. After a two-day trial, on June 20, 1967, Ali was convicted of refusing induction and received the maximum sentence, a five-year prison term and a ten-thousand-dollar fine. He was released pending an appeal of the case, but in the meantime his passport was taken away. He would not be allowed to leave the country.

Ali was immediately slammed in the press and within a short period of time every state boxing commission revoked Ali's license to box. Unwilling to leave the country to fight overseas, now he wouldn't be fighting in the United States, either. At age twenty-five, Ali's boxing career appeared to be over.

But Ali still needed to make a living. Although he had earned hundreds of thousands of dollars, he wasn't a wealthy man. He had never been particularly concerned about money and had given much of his fortune away, a great deal of it to charities. But he was also prone to falling for hard-luck stories and gave money to people he barely knew. A brief marriage in 1965 left him with alimony payments to make, and in August 1967 he married again, this time to a member of the Nation of Islam, Belinda Boyd.

The year 1967 saw opposition to the war spread, particularly on college campuses, where the civil-rights movement also enjoyed wide support. To many young people, black and white, Ali was a hero, someone who had stood up for his principles without concern over the personal cost. He accepted offers to give speeches at colleges, which allowed him to earn some money. But as he spoke out more and more against the war and in favor of civil rights, his chances of returning to the ring seemed ever dimmer.

Ali struggled to make ends meet and to remain in the public eye. He participated in a short film about his life and even appeared briefly in a Broadway musical, *Buck White*. Although the show did not succeed, Ali received good reviews. But everybody knew that all Ali really wanted to do was return to the boxing ring.

Nineteen sixty-eight was one of the most tumultuous years in recent American history. Opposition to the war increased dramatically. On April 4, 1968, Martin Luther King was assassinated, and riots broke out in many American cities. Only two months later,

71

on June 5, anti-war presidential candidate Bobby Kennedy was also assassinated. Meanwhile, the Vietnam War dragged on with no end in sight. Nearly every week some kind of massive protest was held.

Large numbers of Americans began to turn against the Vietnam War and to support the civil-rights movement. The positions held by Muhammad Ali began to appear less extreme. Sportswriters, other members of the media, and the American public slowly started to view Ali in a new light. At the cost of millions of dollars and possibly his career and even his freedom, he had stuck to his convictions. Even those who still disagreed with his political views stopped questioning Ali's sincerity.

Meanwhile, the tournament to name a new heavyweight champion took place. By 1969, Joe Frazier and Jimmy Ellis emerged as the two contenders for the title.

That same year, Ali and the Nation of Islam began to have some differences. Early in the year, in an interview with television commentator Howard Cosell, Ali admitted that he wanted to return to the ring. Although the Nation of Islam had put up with Ali's boxing career, Elijah Muhammad had always held professional athletics in disdain. He had given approval for Ali to box before only because of the publicity it brought to the Nation. But now that Ali was banned from boxing, Elijah Muhammad believed Ali should turn his attention elsewhere. After the Cosell interview, he banished Ali from the church for a year. That marked the beginning of what would eventually lead to a break between Ali and the Nation as Ali's personal religious beliefs began to evolve into a more orthodox version of Islam.

Every few months someone tried to come up with a scheme to stage a boxing match for Ali, only to have those plans fall through when state boxing commissions continued to refuse to license him. On February 16, 1970, Joe Frazier defeated Jimmy Ellis to capture the heavyweight title. But in the minds of many, the title still belonged to Ali.

Shortly after Frazier's victory, the mayor of Atlanta, Georgia, sensing that feelings toward Ali were changing, announced that the city would host him in the ring. The state of Georgia didn't have a boxing commission, so it was impossible for the bout to be stopped. Ali's opponent would be Jerry Quarry, a tough fighter from California who had given both Jimmy Ellis and Joe Frazier serious competition.

Ali was thrilled that he would have the opportunity to box again. But no one, not even him, knew what to expect upon his return. No top athlete in any sport had ever taken three years off and then returned to the top. But that was precisely what Muhammad Ali planned to do.

★ CHAPTER NINE ★

1970

Return of the Greatest

Jerry Quarry was a tough opponent for any fighter to face any time, even more so after a three-year layoff. Ali would have preferred to work his way into shape by fighting several bouts against boxers less skilled and less accomplished before taking on a top contender, but he didn't have a choice.

Ali was now twenty-eight years old. Jerry Quarry, at age twenty-five, was the first professional fighter Ali ever faced who was younger than he — that's how long Ali had been away from the sport.

Although Ali had stayed in relatively good shape during his time away from boxing, he still needed to work hard to prepare himself for Quarry. He went to Georgia to train for the fight and set up camp at a cabin owned by a Georgia politician. He ran many miles each day, jumped rope, watched what he ate, and sparred round after round. Quarry was a dangerous puncher, and if Ali wasn't in top shape he knew he could easily lose the bout. If that happened, he knew he might never receive another opportunity to fight.

But it was hard for Ali to remain focused. There were still some people who didn't want him to return to the ring and others who were against him simply because he was African American. Men drove by his cabin and fired guns, and he received hate-filled letters. On one occasion Ali received a package that contained a dead animal. The message was clear: by remaining in Georgia for the fight, Ali was risking his life. But he had waited for this opportunity too long to back down. He refused to be intimidated and tried to stay focused on the fight.

Since Quarry was white and Ali was African American, some people tried to make the match into a battle between the two races. But neither Ali nor Quarry wanted any part of that. As far as each man was concerned, he was facing another boxer, a man who already had his respect.

The bout was important not just to Ali, but to all his supporters, particularly those in the African American community. During his exile from boxing, Ali had become a hero. As the fight approached famous African Americans from all over the country descended on Atlanta to watch the match. Even Coretta Scott King, Martin Luther King's widow, attended.

The arena filled quickly on the evening of October 26, 1970. The two fighters were introduced to the crowd. Quarry received polite applause and a few *boo*s. But when Ali was introduced the crowd roared and welcomed him back like a long-lost friend.

Dressed in white trunks and white shoes, Ali appeared to be in fine shape, and when the bell rang to start the fight, he immediately went on the attack.

He danced across the ring as the crowd roared its approval, firing jabs in Quarry's face and then dancing away. Clearly, Ali was the much quicker man.

He won the first round easily, but in the second — perhaps tired out from his awesome performance in round one — he slowed. Quarry moved in and threw a big hook to Ali's ribs. Before the layoff Ali probably would have been able to slip away or deflect the body blow. He was in great shape, but his reflexes just weren't the same as they used to be. The long break had cost him his precious and unique gift. The punch found its target and the air rushed from Ali's lungs. He was hurt, and for the rest of the round he tried to keep away from Quarry, who was becoming more confident with each punch.

In round three Quarry went after Ali as if he sensed that the former champion had slowed. The crowd gasped as Ali, flat-footed, failed to slip Quarry's punches.

Then *boom!* Ali turned the fight around. He threw a flurry of punches, stopping Quarry in his tracks and causing the boxer to lower his head and cover his face with his gloves. When the two boxers separated, a huge gash had opened on Quarry's eyebrow and blood rushed down his face.

At the end of the round, the referee called for a doctor to examine Quarry's cut, but the doctor, inexplicably, couldn't be located. The referee took a look and was shocked by what he saw.

Most cuts in boxing are caused when swollen tissue is struck, for at the end of a punch boxers are taught to snap and twist their fist, which can tear the skin, particularly when it is swollen and tight. But this cut was different.

Quarry's face wasn't swollen, yet one of Ali's punches had managed to rip the skin on Quarry's eyebrow. The referee looked at the cut and saw bone. There was no way to stop the bleeding. He instantly stopped the fight.

Ali was back! He wasn't the same fighter he had been before his exile, but he was clearly still dangerous.

Since Ali was in shape and had emerged from the fight unhurt, an attempt was made to schedule another match, this time against Argentine contender Oscar Bonavena. A promoter wanted Ali and Bonavena to fight on December 7 in New York, at Madison Square Garden.

The New York State Boxing Commission refused to sanction the bout. But a civil-rights group, the National Association for the Advancement of Colored People, or NAACP, took the state to court, arguing that Ali's constitutional rights were being violated. Even as his court case was pending appeal, the state of New York allowed dozens of convicted felons to fight.

Finally, the court ruled in Ali's favor. The fight was on.

Bonavena was an awkward fighter. He didn't move much, preferring to slug it out. For most of fifteen long rounds Bonavena stood his ground. Every time Ali moved in to attack, Bonavena counterpunched.

Observers noticed that Ali was absorbing punches, something he'd never done before. Bonavena hoped to tire Ali out and then get lucky.

Entering the fifteenth round, the fight was close. It appeared as if Ali might lose for the first time in his professional career. Bonavena's trainer, Gil Clancy, later described the way they fought the fifteenth round as being like two "Golden Gloves kids" standing toe to toe, punching each other as hard and fast as possible.

But Ali was not ready to lose. All of a sudden he caught Bonavena with a gigantic left hook to the chin, and the Argentine fighter went down.

He got back up after a ten-count but was almost helpless. Before the end of the fifteenth round Ali knocked him down twice more and won the fight on a TKO.

The court decision in New York had opened the door for Ali to resume his career, at least in New York. Although Joe Frazier held the championship belt, in the minds of many Ali was still number one. Hard-core boxing fans wanted to see Ali fight Frazier.

Apart from the color of his skin, Joe Frazier was as different from Muhammad Ali as a man could be. His personality, both in the ring and out of it, was the complete opposite. Ali liked to talk. Frazier did not. Ali was flashy. Frazier was workmanlike and shy. Ali had been raised rather comfortably in the middle class. Joe Frazier's father was a poor sharecropper and Joe was one of fourteen children. Ali was outspoken in regard to race and politics. Frazier was much more conservative in expressing his opinions. Ali liked to dance in the ring. Joe Frazier just plodded on relentlessly. He earned the nickname Smokin' Joe because he fought like a small, powerful engine that never stopped. Boxing fans found the contrast in styles intriguing.

Ali had been acquainted with Frazier for several years. He knew Frazier was an emerging heavyweight and that at some point they would likely meet in the ring. While the two fighters weren't close, they were friendly toward each other.

Late in 1969, at a radio interview in Philadelphia, where Frazier lived and trained, Ali got everyone's attention — particularly Joe Frazier's. During the interview, Ali called Frazier a "coward" and a "chump" and, worst of all, an "Uncle Tom," a derogatory term that refers to a submissive slave and is very offensive to African Americans. Ali then challenged Frazier to prove he wasn't a coward by showing up at a local gym in an hour to settle the matter.

Joe Frazier was listening to Ali's rant from his own gym. He felt humiliated in his hometown and smashed the radio with his foot. He raced to the other gym, where police had to separate the two men. The next day the two fighters appeared together on a television show, and after the show the two men scuffled.

That night Frazier paid Ali a visit. He was still angry. Ali tried to explain that he had said what he did "just for fun," but Frazier didn't believe him and criticized Ali for being a Muslim. The goodwill between the two fighters disappeared, and they genuinely began to dislike each other.

Over the next few months Ali continued to insult Frazier, saying his chances of beating him were "slim and none."

Although his antics had cost him his friendship

with Frazier, it worked. On December 30, 1970, the two fighters signed a contract for a title fight to take place on March 8, 1971, at Madison Square Garden in New York. The promoters dubbed the bout the Fight of the Century and guaranteed each fighter $2.5 million dollars, making it the most lucrative match in the history of boxing at the time and the single biggest payday up to that point in the history of sports.

Muhammad Ali would have a chance to take back the title — the one he felt was rightfully his.

★ CHAPTER TEN ★
1971

Fights of the Century

No one was ever better at pre-fight promotion than Muhammad Ali. He had learned his lesson from Gorgeous George years before. Ali had created an intense rivalry between himself and Frazier, one that left fans polarized. Ali fans hated Frazier, and Frazier fans — many of whom had been offended by Ali's choice of words — hated Ali.

In the weeks before the fight, Ali was relentless, taking every opportunity to insult Frazier, even calling fans of Frazier "Uncle Toms." Frazier, although much less vocal when compared to Ali, nevertheless made his few words bite. He refused to call his opponent by his name and offended Ali by referring to him as "Clay."

Madison Square Garden quickly sold out, and more than 300 million tickets were sold in forty-six different countries for the chance to watch the fight in theaters on closed-circuit television. By the day of the fight anticipation was incredible. Never before had a boxing match been such a worldwide event. Frazier was a narrow favorite.

At the start of the fight both fighters had a plan. Ali knew he was faster and planned to "float like a butterfly and sting like a bee," forcing Frazier to chase after him. Ali thought Frazier would tire, after which he could be hit. He even composed a poem for the fight that explained his strategy: "Joe's gonna come out smokin' / But I ain't gonna be jokin' / I'll be pickin' and pokin' / Pouring water on his smokin' / This might shock and amaze ya / But I'm gonna destroy Joe Frazier."

But Frazier had a plan, too. He had channeled his anger at Ali into his training and was in great shape. He had studied Ali's fights against Quarry and Bonavena and realized that Ali couldn't move the way he had before the layoff. He planned to exhaust Ali by punishing him with body shots to the hips and midsection. Once Ali was unable to dance, Frazier was confident he could hit him.

At the start of the fight, Frazier came out smokin',

and Ali was pickin' and pokin'. For the first couple rounds Ali danced and jabbed, sometimes dropping his hands and sticking out his chin, daring Frazier to hit him and making Frazier look foolish while appearing to hit Frazier at will. Between rounds Ali didn't even bother to sit on his stool, as if he didn't need the rest.

But Frazier refused to get frustrated. He stuck with his plan. In the third round Ali began to slow as Frazier found his range and started landing shots. Ali tried to laugh them off, leaning against the ropes and joking and talking as Frazier threw punch after punch.

By the middle of the fight, it was clear that Frazier's blows were beginning to take effect. He kept pinning Ali against the ropes, and for the first time anyone could remember, Ali seemed unable to dance away. After ten rounds the fight was still up for grabs.

The eleventh round has become one of the most famous battles in boxing history and is often referred to as the Gruesome Eleventh. Frazier rocked Ali and his legs began to wobble. No one had ever seen Ali hurt so badly. He was almost defenseless in the face of Frazier's onslaught.

Although Ali was no longer as quick as he had been, he was stronger. The Bonavena fight had taught him that he could withstand a punch. He took everything Frazier had and somehow remained on his feet.

Now in the twelfth round, Frazier began to show the effects of fatigue as Ali rallied. The crowd was going crazy. Never before had they seen two fighters give such an incredible effort.

By the fifteenth, and final, round both fighters looked beaten. Ali was unsteady on his feet and Frazier's face was grotesquely swollen. Both men were now fighting on willpower alone. The winner of the fifteenth round would take the fight.

Then *boom!* Frazier unleashed a thunderous left hook, almost leaving his feet to throw it. Ali was too tired to get out of the way. The punch caught him flush on the side of the head, and his legs collapsed as he fell on his back. Ali was down!

Somehow he managed to stagger to his feet, but his will was gone. Although he remained upright for the remainder of the fight, it was clear that Joe Frazier had given Ali the first defeat of his professional career. A few moments later it was made official.

The judges announced Frazier's win with a unanimous decision.

As far as the fans were concerned, the Fight of the Century had lived up to the hype. But the match had taken a tremendous toll on both Frazier and Ali. At the post-fight press conference both had trouble speaking. In fact, the two fighters were beaten so badly each had to spend time in the hospital afterward — Ali staying overnight, while Frazier stayed for several weeks.

But Ali was still fighting another battle. In April, just weeks after the fight and more than four years after the original hearing, his court case over his refusal to be inducted into the Army was finally going to be argued before the United States Supreme Court. If he lost he would have to go to jail.

The justices heard arguments from Ali's attorneys, and the prosecution then met to consider the question. One of the nine justices, Thurgood Marshall, had to recuse himself, or step down from the case, because he had been the prosecutor when Ali was first charged.

The court initially voted to uphold Ali's conviction. Then one of the judges changed his mind after doing some research on the Nation of Islam, and the vote was a 4–4 tie — but they had to rule one way or the other. Then Justice Potter Stewart found a mistake in the paperwork filed by the prosecution. When he alerted his colleagues, they had no choice but to vote unanimously in Ali's favor. All charges were dismissed. Ali would not go to jail. Nor would he have to join the Army.

Ali may have lost boxing's Fight of the Century, but he had won his personal Fight of the Century in a court of law. For the first time in more than four years he was a free man, able to pursue his career in the United States and, with the return of his passport, anywhere else in the world.

As rewarding as the victory was, Ali knew there was only one thing that would truly put his career back on track. He immediately issued a challenge to Joe Frazier calling for a rematch. To return to the top, he had to win back his title as heavyweight champion of the world.

☆ CHAPTER ELEVEN ☆

1972–1974

A Rematch and a Rumble

Now that his court case was no longer hanging over his head, Ali was able to concentrate on his career again. He fought nine times over the next eighteen months, staying sharp while waiting for Joe Frazier to grant him a rematch. Meanwhile, Frazier was determined to make Ali wait. He fought a series of easy fights as well.

But Joe Frazier and Muhammad Ali weren't the only two heavyweights in boxing, and knowledge-able observers noted that each fighter seemed to have slipped a little since their epic battle. The future of the heavyweight division seemed to belong to George Foreman. Since winning the gold medal for the United States at the 1968 Olympics, George Foreman had wreaked havoc in the heavyweight division. He was undefeated and won nearly every fight by a knockout. Not since Sonny Liston had a heavyweight been so feared for his punching power. By 1973 he had risen so high that champ Joe Frazier was unable to avoid giving him a shot at the title.

Frazier and Foreman met on January 22, 1973, in Jamaica. Foreman made Frazier look small and weak. From the opening bell he dominated the champion, knocking him down six times in two rounds to take the title.

Meanwhile, Ali agreed to fight Ken Norton, who had served as a sparring partner for Frazier, on March 31 of the same year. Norton was a good fighter, but not a contender. Ali didn't take the bout very seriously. He didn't train especially hard, and after suffering a sprained ankle while playing golf he slacked off even more.

The bout attracted so little interest that it was televised for free on national TV. From the start Norton seemed to trouble Ali. He fought awkwardly, which put Ali on the defensive. In the second round Norton backed Ali up against the ropes, then *wham!* hit him on the jaw with a straight right hand.

When Ali went back to his corner at the end of the round, he was bleeding from inside his mouth. The right hand had broken his jaw!

Ali's cornermen wanted him to quit, but Ali refused. Despite the broken jaw, and in incredible pain, he continued the fight, losing on points.

It was valiant effort. Still, many observers assumed after the loss that Ali was on the way down. If he couldn't beat Ken Norton, how could he ever beat George Foreman and regain the title? Ali took six months off to recover. Then he beat Norton in a tough rematch.

There was still intense interest in a rematch between Frazier and Ali, and now that neither man was the champion there was no reason for the two to avoid each another. Ali and Frazier signed a contract to fight a rematch at Madison Square Garden on January 28, 1974.

Once again the two men taunted each other before the fight. Frazier kept referring to Ali as "Clay," and Ali kept calling Frazier "ignorant." During a joint television appearance only five days before the fight, both men took offense at what the other said and scuffled again, each earning a $5,000 fine.

This time Ali was the narrow favorite. He was in better shape than he had been in their first bout and he fought a smarter fight. He stayed off the ropes, hit Frazier with combinations of punches, and then tied him up before Frazier could hurt him. Although the fight lacked the excitement of their earlier bout — neither man was knocked down — for Ali, the result was much easier to take. He beat Frazier on points and won in a unanimous decision. Frazier immediately called for a rematch.

But Ali's win put him on a collision course with George Foreman. Few thought Ali could beat Foreman, whose record stood at 40–0 with thirty-seven knockouts. But just as everyone in the world had wanted to see the first match between Ali and Frazier, everyone now wanted to see Ali and Foreman face off. Until Foreman beat Ali, many people would refuse to recognize him as a true champion.

Flamboyant boxing promoter Don King turned the fight into a sporting spectacle unlike any other the world had ever seen. The president of the African nation of Zaire, a dictator named Mobuto Sese Seko — whom everyone just called Mobuto — wanted to host the fight to generate publicity for his nation.

King agreed and scheduled Ali and Foreman to meet on September 25, 1974, for the incredible purse of $5 million dollars each. The Rumble in the Jungle was on.

Zaire was a poor country wracked by poverty and internal strife. But Mobuto and King were determined to put on a show. Ali and Foreman both arrived in Kinshasa, the capital, several weeks before the fight to train. King even scheduled a big concert featuring the world's best entertainers of African descent. In advance of the fight Mobuto arrested all his enemies and anyone else he didn't want the world to see to give the impression that Zaire was a peaceful place.

Although many members of the media were uncomfortable with the conditions in the developing country, Ali loved Zaire. Every day he walked the streets and was surrounded by fans — African fans. They followed him, shouting, "Ali, Ali, *bomaye!*" which means, "Ali, kill him!" The Zairean people embraced Ali as a hero, as a man who had stood up to the United States government and had won. He was much more popular than George Foreman.

Most observers thought that was where Ali's edge

stopped. Although he called Foreman a "mummy" and a "big old bully" and even wrote a poem that began, "Float like a butterfly, sting like a bee, / His hands can't hit what his eyes can't see," most boxing writers and fans thought Foreman was far too powerful for Ali and expected a short fight. After all, Foreman had knocked out Joe Frazier easily, and Ali had not been able to knock Frazier down. Even Foreman thought he would have an easy fight. He was a 3–1 favorite.

Eight days before the fight, Foreman suffered a cut over his eye while sparring. The fight was postponed until October 30 and the Zairean government, afraid the delay would cause the fight to be taken elsewhere, actually warned both Foreman and Ali that it would be "unwise" — and unsafe — if either man tried to leave the country.

By October 30, interest in the fight was at fever pitch. The bout was scheduled for 4:00 a.m., Zairean time, to accommodate American theaters. The predawn air was warm and humid. The two men fought outside in a covered arena before thousands of fans. Many had been up all night partying. They chanted "Ali, *bomaye!*" over and over again.

At the opening bell Ali started dancing and Foreman started stalking him. Foreman planned to work inside. In an earlier fight one of his punches had actually broken another fighter's arm. He planned to pound Ali's arms to rob him of his power and then go to the body. He was confident Ali wouldn't last very long.

Angelo Dundee wanted Ali to stay away from Foreman, to dance and stick and jab. He thought Ali's only chance for victory was to stay out of harm's way early, hope Foreman got tired, and win the fight in the final rounds.

In the first round, both men stuck to their plans. But in the humidity, Ali realized he couldn't dance the entire fight. He exchanged some big punches with Foreman in the middle of the ring. He felt his opponent's power, but he also realized that he could beat him to the punch. Ali still had the fastest hands in the heavyweight division.

Now he showed why he was a true champion. After preparing to fight one way for months, he instantly changed strategy.

In the second round he stopped dancing. In fact, he almost stopped fighting. He leaned far back against the ropes, covered his face and head with his gloves, and let Foreman pound away, a strategy he later called the rope-a-dope.

Angelo Dundee later admitted he felt "sick" as he watched Ali endure the punishment. Foreman hit him with every punch he had. All Ali did was lean back and take it, talking the entire time, egging Foreman on, trying to get him to punch harder and harder. "Is that all you have?" Ali kept asking. "They told me you could punch." Foreman just got madder and madder and punched harder and harder.

Ali's corner begged him to fight back, but Ali insisted, "I know what I'm doing." Most fans and observers were puzzled and thought Ali was so afraid of Foreman he wasn't going to fight at all.

Ali kept this up for seven long rounds, all of which he lost. But in the eighth round the wisdom of his approach became obvious.

Foreman was exhausted. His punches were beginning to slow and lose their power. Ali was still fresh.

All of a sudden Ali broke away from the ropes and started dancing, darting in and out, throwing lightning-quick jabs at Foreman's head. The champion moved as if he were in quicksand. His arms were in slow motion. He couldn't block any of Ali's punches.

The crowd went crazy and the chants of "Ali, *bo-maye!*" grew louder and louder. Then Ali moved in. He hit Foreman with overhand rights and sweeping lefts, knocking him back and forth like a stuffed animal.

Foreman was defenseless. Suddenly he fell like a big tree face first into the center of the ring. The referee counted him out. Ali was the winner by a knockout!

Ten years after beating Sonny Liston to win the title for the first time, and seven years after being stripped of his title, Muhammad Ali was again the undisputed heavyweight champion of the world.

★ CHAPTER TWELVE ★

1975–1981

The Thrilla in Manila and After

In the months after Foreman's defeat, the world began to agree with what Ali had been saying all along.
Perhaps he was "the greatest champion of all times."
When he was champion in the 1960s, he was still a
young man and had won the title with his breath-
taking speed and his ability to dance and slip punches
like no one else. Nearly a decade later, as his own
boxing skills had diminished, he had transformed
himself. Now he could apparently fight any style, any
time. The younger Ali rarely got hit, but as an older
fighter Ali learned to take a punch and still figure
out a way to win. He was clearly the most intelligent
boxer ever to hold the title.

His career had come full circle. Meanwhile, the
United States had turned a hundred and eighty de-
grees on the issues that had nearly cost Ali his career.

The Vietnam War ended in 1975 when the United States finally withdrew. Civil rights were now the law of the land, and African Americans were guaranteed equal treatment by the government. Ali, whose ideas and outspokenness had once made him appear radical, was now mainstream. President Gerald Ford even invited him to visit the White House.

In early 1975 Elijah Muhammad died, and under the leadership of his son Wallace, the Nation of Islam began to change. Instead of preaching racial separatism, it began to promote more mainstream Islamic values, coming out in favor of tolerance and brotherhood. Although the change eventually led to a split in the Nation, Ali embraced this new direction. After all, in many ways his entire public life had been about bringing people together from the very beginning.

Now that he was champion again, every other contender wanted to take a shot at him. Ali didn't run from anyone; that simply wasn't his style. In the first half of 1975 he fought three more times, winning tough fights against Chuck Wepner, Ron Lyle, and Joe Bugner.

But there was still Joe Frazier. The men had split their two earlier fights. Both wanted to fight one more time to decide, forever, who was the better boxer. Besides, Frazier also wanted a shot at the title. Another dictator, Ferdinand Marcos of the Philippines, wanted to host the fight. The two boxers agreed to meet there on October 1, 1975.

Once again, Ali and Frazier viciously insulted each other in the days before the fight. They weren't trying to drum up more interest in their battle. There was plenty of that already. They simply disliked each other. In his poem about the match Ali referred to the fight as the Thrilla in Manila — the capital of the Philippines — and called Frazier a "gorilla," a term offensive to people of African descent. Frazier called Ali a "half-breed," something equally offensive. Both men put everything they had into their training.

For the two boxers, the fight unfolded like a personal battle, even though it would be fought in public. Neither cared much about trying to win on points. Both just wanted to beat the other man in any way possible.

In the eyes of many, the Thrilla in Manila is the greatest match in boxing history. Fought in 110-degree heat in the middle of the night, both men simply stood toe to toe for fourteen long rounds and exchanged punches in a battle of wills. In the end the man with the most courage would win the fight.

In the early rounds, Ali danced and jabbed and buckled Frazier's legs several times, but he soon tired. Then Frazier found his range and pounded Ali with thunderous punches, some of which caused him to leave his feet. Neither fighter bothered with strategy. Each just aimed for the head and went for the knockout, talking to the other the whole time, throwing insults with every punch.

In the seventh round it was obvious that each man was exhausted and could barely move his legs. They just stood in front of each other and exchanged blows that would have knocked out lesser fighters.

By the twelfth round Frazier seemed to have the advantage. For the last few rounds he'd been able to back Ali into a corner and had thrown more punches. It was reminiscent of their first fight. Many people expected Ali to fall.

But Ali had fought too many battles inside and

outside the ring to give up. From somewhere deep inside he summoned the strength to fight back. He drew on reserves of energy no one knew he had and started taking the fight to Frazier again. In the thirteenth round he took command, and a jolting left hook sent Frazier's mouthpiece flying. The tide had turned.

In round fourteen Frazier's face was a mess, his left eye virtually swollen shut. Ali sent punch after punch into his opponent's face as Frazier, nearly blinded, desperately tried to fight back, pawing at an opponent he could barely see.

At the end of the round Frazier slumped in his corner. His trainer, Eddie Futch, saw that his left eye was completely closed and that now his right eye was so swollen that only a small slit remained.

Ali, in his corner, was also badly hurt. His entire face was puffy and he was exhausted. Neither man really looked as if he could — or should — continue. Each had absorbed as much punishment as any two boxers ever had.

Futch was afraid that if the fight continued, Frazier would be seriously injured. Over the protests of Frazier, Futch threw in the towel, ending the fight.

Ali did not celebrate — he didn't have the energy for that. He stood up and then slumped to the floor with exhaustion. He had won the fight — barely.

Each fighter left the ring feeling greater respect for the other. "I hit him with punches that would bring down the walls of a city," Frazier said later. "Lordy, he's great." Ali later explained, "It was like death. Closest thing to dyin' that I know of." People who had seen the bout knew they had witnessed a battle of athleticism, determination, and will rarely seen before.

The victory secured Ali's legendary status. His popularity skyrocketed. Even those who had never liked the way he acted or the things he said admired him for his ability.

But the fight took a devastating toll on each man. Neither would ever be the same again, either in the ring or out of it. Simply put, the human body is not meant to take such repeated punishment. In their third fight each man crossed a line.

Yet Ali would not stop fighting. By beating Frazier and surviving, he seemed like some kind of comic-book superhero. Over the next two years he fought six more times. Although he won all six fights, four went to fifteen rounds. Ali still had the skills to win, but it was becoming much harder for him to knock out his opponent, and in each fight he absorbed more and more punishment. Those around him began to tell Ali that it was time for him to retire before boxing took a permanent toll on his health.

Boxing can be a safe sport, but it can also be dangerous. A single punch can — and has — caused boxers to die. The accumulation of punches in a career often causes brain damage. Many old fighters become punch-drunk, a medical malady known as dementia pugilistica, brain damage caused by bleeding from repeated blows to the head. The history of boxing is littered with former champions who fought too long, took too many blows, and ended up unable to take care of themselves. No one who admired Ali wanted to see this happen to him.

Ali, however, felt invincible. And he still needed the money, for he remained unskilled at managing his finances and he supported a growing entourage of assistants and hangers-on. He kept on taking fights.

On February 15, 1978, he fought former Olympic champion Leon Spinks. Spinks wasn't a very good fighter, but when Ali entered the ring, neither was he. His reflexes were gone; his punches, slow; and he couldn't get to Spinks.

In desperation he even resorted to the rope-a-dope maneuver again. This time it didn't work. Spinks didn't tire and Ali couldn't counterpunch effectively. He lost the fight on a decision.

But Ali was determined not to retire without the heavyweight title. He went back into training and in September fought Spinks again. Since winning the title, Spinks, an undisciplined man, had run wild, drinking and doing drugs. He was in poor shape when the two met for the second time.

This time Ali fought a smarter fight and Spinks hardly fought at all. Ali regained his title in a decision to become the first heavyweight champion to win the title three times.

Then, at last, it was time to stop. Ali himself said he would be a "fool" if he fought again, and ten months later he announced his retirement, voluntarily giving up his title. "I'm getting out of boxing," he said. "Boxing was the dressing room, a preliminary for the big fight for humanity, racial justice, freedom, and human rights."

But professional athletes become so accustomed to success and life in the spotlight that it is difficult for them to stop. Very few who retire while at the top manage to stay retired.

Unfortunately, Muhammad Ali was no different. He traveled the world promoting charitable causes, but he missed boxing. And despite earning millions of dollars, he was running out of money as he discovered that many of the people around him had taken advantage of his generosity.

In the meantime, one of Ali's former sparring partners, Larry Holmes, had won the heavyweight title. Ali remembered how he had been able to dominate Holmes during training. He thought he could win the title a fourth time.

It was a bad idea. Already people were beginning to notice that Ali's speech was beginning to slur and his hands trembled. Nevertheless, he fought Holmes in 1980.

It wasn't a close match. Ali had nothing. Holmes even took it easy on the champion, whom he considered a hero. The fight was finally stopped after ten rounds. Holmes had won every round.

Incredibly, Ali refused to believe he was finished. One year later, in 1981, at age thirty-nine, he fought again, taking on a journeyman named Trevor Berbick.

Berbick wasn't a very good fighter, but compared to him Ali looked terrible. After ten rounds the fight was stopped and Berbick was declared the winner.

This time Ali retired for good. "I'm finished," he said. But although he was finished with boxing, Muhammad Ali still had more to accomplish.

✷ CHAPTER THIRTEEN ✷

1981–Present

The Final Lesson

Over the next few years Ali tried to withdraw from the spotlight and enjoy retirement. He doted on his nine children. He spent his time either at his home in Michigan, visiting with his parents in Louisville, or traveling the world as sort of a goodwill ambassador. He became ever more religious, practicing orthodox Islam and praying five times a day. Although he was still dogged by financial problems, he slowly began to take control of that part of his life, and the lucrative sports-memorabilia market promised him a steady source of income from signing autographs, if he chose to pursue it.

But by 1984 his physical condition was deteriorating. He found it difficult to speak, to concentrate, and to sleep, and his body began developing tremors. He underwent a thorough medical examination. Many of those around him were afraid that he was suffering from dementia pugilistica.

The doctors determined that Ali was ill but that he was not punch-drunk. He was diagnosed with a disease known as Parkinson's syndrome. This syndrome should not be confused with Parkinson's disease, a hereditary nerve disease that is eventually fatal. While Parkinson's syndrome mimics many of the symptoms of Parkinson's disease, such as difficulty walking and speaking and the presence of trembling hands, it doesn't affect intelligence and is not life threatening.

The root cause of Parkinson's syndrome, in the minds of most doctors, was Ali's boxing career. The continued trauma of taking blows to the head caused too many brain cells to die.

Fortunately, a great deal of research on the malady is being done. However, while medication can help, the damage is irreversible.

Remarkably, Ali seemed to accept his fate without complaint and with uncommon grace. He turned to Islam for comfort and instead of complaining about his fate or being wracked with regret, he chose to view it as part of Allah's plan for him. His entire life demonstrates the way a person can grow over a lifetime. The brash, self-centered young man whose life was built around violence has become a person who brings others together and is now focused on peace and brotherhood. Ali isn't shy about appearing in public and continues to keep up a busy schedule. Each day he signs hundreds of Islamic pamphlets and gives them to everyone he meets, gently preaching tolerance.

For many it is painful to see Ali, once known for his rapid-fire speech, now strugging to form words. But when Ali does speak today, he makes the most of it, usually saying something that makes people either stop and think about their lives or cracking a joke, showing that his mind is still sharp and clear.

He loves to do magic tricks, particularly for children, including one remarkable trick that makes it appear as if he is levitating. Then he explains that Allah teaches people not to deceive and reveals how the trick is done. He also likes to pull gentle practical jokes. One of his favorites, which he's been known to do while being interviewed by a writer, is to pretend to fall asleep and then start throwing punches as if dreaming. When he finally throws one that stops just inches from his companion's face, Ali will open his eyes wide and say, "Fooled you, didn't I?"

In 1986 Ali divorced his third wife, Veronica Porche, and married Lonnie Williams, whom he had known since 1962. Muhammad and Lonnie have adopted two children. She takes great care of her husband and has helped to make certain that he is financially secure. Even now they spend nearly three hundred days a year traveling. As Ali has grown older he has become an even more beloved figure to people from all over the world. His appeal was never made more obvious than at the 1996 Olympic Games in Atlanta.

A torch is always carried from the site of the last Olympic Games to the next one, and the lighting of the torch symbolizes the start of the Olympics. American officials kept secret the identity of the person who would light the torch at the 1996 opening ceremony.

Evander Holyfield, a former heavyweight-boxing champion and Olympic medalist, carried the torch into the stadium. He passed it off to gold-medalist swimmer Janet Evans. She climbed a long, narrow flight of stars to the top of the stadium.

When she reached the peak, a figure dressed in white stepped from the shadows. It was Muhammad Ali.

She passed him the torch, and despite the trembling caused by Parkinson's syndrome Ali held the torch high and proud over his head.

The crowd roared and cheered. Many people broke into tears. No other human being on earth was known and cared for by so many people. Millions of people all over the world saw in Ali the true message of the Olympics: the uniting of people of all colors and cultures. Then Ali slowly bent down and ever so gently lit the Olympic flame. It burned brightly, and Ali, the Greatest, basked in its glow.

Muhammad Ali's Professional Record

Year	Date	Opponent	Site	Result	Title
1960	October 29	Tunney Hunsaker	Louisville	W 6	
	December 27	Herb Siler	Miami Beach	KO 4	
1961	January 17	Anthony Sperti	Miami Beach	KO 3	
	February 7	Jim Robinson	Miami Beach	KO 1	
	February 21	Donnie Fleeman	Miami Beach	KO 7	
	April 19	Lamar Clark	Louisville	KO 2	
	June 26	Duke Sabedong	Las Vegas	W 10	
	July 22	Alonzo Johnson	Louisville	W 10	
	October 7	Alex Miteff	Louisville	KO 6	
	November 29	Willi Besmanoff	Louisville	KO 7	
1962	February 10	Sonny Banks	New York	KO 4	
	February 28	Don Warner	Miami Beach	KO 4	
	April 23	George Logan	Los Angeles	KO 4	
	May 19	Billy Daniels	New York	KO 7	
	July 20	Alejandro Lavorante	Los Angeles	KO 5	
	November 15	Archie Moore	Los Angeles	KO 4	
1963	January 24	Charlie Powell	Pittsburgh	KO 3	
	March 13	Doug Jones	New York	W 10	
	June 18	Henry Cooper	London	KO 5	
1964	February 25	Sonny Liston	Miami Beach	KO 7	World

Year	Date	Opponent	Site	Result	Title
1965	May 25	Sonny Liston	Lewiston, ME	KO 1	World
	November 22	Floyd Patterson	Las Vegas	KO 12	World
1966	March 29	George Chuvalo	Toronto	W 15	World
	May 21	Henry Cooper	London	KO 6	World
	August 6	Brian London	London	KO 3	World
	September 10	Karl Mildenberger	Frankfurt, Germany	KO 12	World
	November 14	Cleveland Williams	Houston	KO 3	World
1967	February 6	Ernie Terrell	Houston	W 15	World
	March 22	Zora Folley	New York	KO 7	World
1970	October 26	Jerry Quarry	Atlanta	KO 3	
	December 7	Oscar Bonavena	New York	KO 15	
1971	March 8	Joe Frazier	New York	L 15	World
	July 26	Jimmy Ellis	Houston	KO 12	NABF
	November 17	Buster Mathis	Houston	W 12	NABF
	December 26	Jürgen Blin	Zurich, Switzerland	KO 7	
1972	April 1	Mac Foster	Tokyo, Japan	W 15	
	May 1	George Chuvalo	Vancouver	W 12	NABF
	June 27	Jerry Quarry	Las Vegas	KO 7	NABF
	July 19	Alvin Lewis	Dublin, Ireland	KO 11	
	September 20	Floyd Patterson	New York	KO 7	NABF

Year	Date	Opponent	Site	Result	Title
1972	November 21	Bob Foster	Stateline, NV	KO 8	NABF
1973	February 14	Joe Bugner	Las Vegas	W 12	
	March 31	Ken Norton	San Diego	L 12	NABF
	September 10	Ken Norton	Los Angeles	W 12	NABF
	October 21	Rudy Lubbers	Jakarta, Indonesia	W 12	
1974	January 28	Joe Frazier	New York	W 12	NABF
	October 30	George Foreman	Kinshasa, Zaire	KO 8	World
1975	March 24	Chuck Wepner	Cleveland	KO 15	World
	May 16	Ron Lyle	Las Vegas	KO 11	World
	June 30	Joe Bugner	Kuala Lumpur, Malaysia	W 15	World
	October 1	Joe Frazier	Manila, Philippines	KO 14	World
1976	February 20	Jean-Pierre Coopman	San Juan, Puerto Rico	KO 5	World
	April 30	Jimmy Young	Landover, MD	W 15	World
	May 24	Richard Dunn	Munich, Germany	KO 5	World
	September 28	Ken Norton	New York	W 15	World
1977	May 16	Alfredo Evangelista	Landover, MD	W 15	World
	September 29	Earnie Shavers	New York	W 15	World
1978	February 15	Leon Spinks	Las Vegas	L 15	World
	September 15	Leon Spinks	New Orleans	W 15	WBA
1980	October 2	Larry Holmes	Las Vegas	KO'd 11	WBC
1981	December 11	Trevor Berbick	Nassau, Bahamas	L 10	

Total: 61 — Won: 56 (91.8%) — Lost: 5 (8.2%) — KOs: 37 (60.7%)

Before Exile: 29 — Won: 29 (100%) — KOs: 23 (79.3%)

After Exile: 32 — Won: 27 (84.4%) — Lost: 5 (15.6%) — KOs: 14 (43.8%)

Championship Bouts: 25 — Won: 22 (88%) — Lost: 3 (12%) — KOs: 14 (56%)

NABF: North American Boxing Federation; WBA: World Boxing Association; WBC: World Boxing Congress

Matt Christopher®

Kobe Bryant	Michael Jordan
Terrell Davis	Lisa Leslie
John Elway	Tara Lipinski
Julie Foudy	Mark McGwire
Jeff Gordon	Greg Maddux
Wayne Gretzky	Hakeem Olajuwon
Ken Griffey Jr.	Alex Rodriguez
Mia Hamm	Briana Scurry
Tony Hawk	Sammy Sosa
Grant Hill	Tiger Woods
Derek Jeter	Steve Young
Randy Johnson	

The #1 Sports Series for Kids

MATT CHRISTOPHER®

Read them all!

All available in paperback from Little, Brown and Company